THE

IN THE QUR'AN AND THE SUNNA

Mustafa Ashour

Dar Al – Taqwa

بسم الله الرحمن الرحيم

Reprinted July 2000

ISBN 1 870582 02 0

Translation : Aisha Bewley

Editorial : Abdalhaqq Bewley & idris Mears

Published by:
Dar Al Taqwa Ltd.
7A Melcombe Street
Baker Street
London NW1 6AE
www.daraltaqwa.com
email : info@daraltaqwa.com

Printed and Bound by :
De-Luxe Printers, London
Tel. : 020 8965 1771
email : de-luxe@talk21.com

CONTENTS

FOREWORD

Praise be to Allah! He has created man from dry clay and created the jinn from smokeless fire and made them invisible to the eyes of men. He has made some of them righteous and some he has led astray and he has not given them any power over man other than in whispering and the allurements of Shaytan.

Blessings and peace be upon Muhammad! Allah has sent him as a mercy to all the worlds and has sent him to all peoples. Passing jinn were drawn by his recitation of the Qur'an and they stopped to listen and when he had finished they went back and conveyed the message to their people.

Allah then revealed to the Prophet:

'A company of the jinn gave ear, then they said,
We have heard a wonderful Qur'an,
guiding to right action.
We believe in it
and we will not associate anyone
with our Lord.' (72:1-2)

I testify that there is no god but Allah alone without partner! I have learned from His faultless Book that Shaytan is a clear enemy to man.

I testify that Muhammad is His slave and messenger! He sent him with the means to well-being for all men. He revealed to him His clear words:

'And say, O my Lord, I seek refuge with You
from the whisperings of Shaytan
and I seek refuge with You, my Lord,
lest they be present with me.' (23:97-98)

May Allah bless him and his family!

The world of the jinn is brimming over with secrets, marvels and wonders and this is what excites people's interest in it.

Detailed research into the term 'jinn' in the Arabic language uncovers an astonishing number of words which refer to them, either directly or indirectly. There are names for the jinn as reality and concept, words which refer generally to their connections with mankind, and phrases used specifically for how they attack men and how they associate with them. The jinn have certain distinguishing features as does their environment.

Accepting the existence of the jinn is an integral part of the deen since the Noble Qur'an indicates the existence of creatures which are called jinn, some of whom are righteous and some of whom are not.

Those who deny the jinn deny the Qur'an. They are denying that there exists beyond the material world an unseen world which has its own special properties as clearly supported by the science of hadith. Only an ignorant person or an unbeliever would deny this!

We as Muslims must hold to what has come from the Lord of the Worlds.

Shaykh ash-Sha'rawi says, 'It is obligatory to believe in the judgments of the deen in unseen matters. It does not matter that we do not fully understand them. Belief has a peak and its peak is to believe in Allah. If you believe in Allah by choice and reach the peak with your intellect, then you accept all that Allah tells you whether or not your intellect can grasp it.'

So this book which Allah has enabled us to write is a clear call to pure tawhid and worship of Allah alone and forbids innovations, superstitions and fables which prevail among people, past and present. It presents the world of the jinn to the reader as it is, being based on the Qur'an, the sunna, traditions and the words of scholars.

The contents cover those matters which concern us as human beings and answer our questions on the subject. I hope I have presented the truth in a simple, straightforward and clear way. The pleasure of Allah is my goal and my success is due only to Allah. I have relied on him and to Him I turn.

Mustafa Ashour
Cairo, Dhu'l-Qa'da, 1407
July, 1986

CHAPTER ONE

THE REALITY AND NATURE OF THE THE WORLD OF THE JINN

Comprising:

Confirmation of the existence of the world of the jinn.
Who are the jinn?
From what are the jinn created?
When were the jinn created?
The types of jinn.
Do the jinn have bodies?
Do the jinn have other names?
Do the jinn have the power to take on forms?
The capabilities and powers of the jinn.
Do the jinn die?
How does Shaytan walk?
What is the time when Shaytan is most frequently present?
Where is the throne of Iblis?
The actions which Iblis did before the sons of Adam.
Is Iblis a jinn or an angel?
Do the jinn feel envy? Can they harm us?

CONFIRMATION OF THE EXISTENCE OF THE WORLD OF THE JINN

Many people, past and present, have disagreed about the existence of the jinn. Some completely reject their existence, whereas some claim that what is meant by the jinn are the evil inclinations and tendencies of the corrupt human soul and likewise that what is meant by angels are good inclinations.

Spiritualists, while they recognise the existence of the jinn, call them lower spirits. They claim that these lower spirits are quick to respond but that their response is weak whereas the celestial spirits are very slow to respond although their response is more powerful.

Some idol worshippers claim that what is meant by jinn are the spirits of the planets.

So it can be seen that most people believe in the existence of the jinn in one form or another.

There are empirical proofs of the existence of the jinn as well as Qur'anic ayats, prophetic hadiths and direct testimony by eyewitnesses.

As for the Qur'anic ayats which indicate the existence of the jinn, they are numerous and we will only quote a few of them:

Allah says,

'I only created the jinn and men to worship Me.' (51:56)

There were certain men of mankind
'who would take refuge with certain men of the jinn
and they increased them in ill nature.' (72:6)

'Say: It has been revealed to me
that a company of the jinn listened...' (72:1)

'We created the jinn before from the fire of hot wind.' (15:27)

There are also a number of hadiths from the Prophet. For instance, the Messenger of Allah, may Allah bless him and grant him peace, said, 'There are three types of jinn. One type flies through the air. Another type consists of snakes and dogs. A third type is based in one place but travels about.' (*This hadith is related by al-Hakam, at-Tabarani and al-Bayhaqi.*)

There are many other hadiths which give absolute proof of the existence of the jinn and we will be mentioning some of them later in this book.

WHO ARE THE JINN?

The jinn are part of Allah's creation, separate from man and the angels, but they share with man certain qualities like intellect, discrimination, freedom and the power to choose between true and false, right and wrong, the good and bad. They are distinct from man in certain essentials, the most important of which is their origin since the basic substance of jinn is not the same as the basic substance of man.

FROM WHAT ARE THE JINN CREATED?

Allah informs us in many ayats that He has created the jinn from fire. For instance, He says,

'We created the jinn before from the fire of hot wind.' (15:27)

He also says,

'He created the jinn from smokeless fire.' (55:15)

Smokeless fire means the tips of flames as Ibn 'Abbas, Mujahid and others have reported. One version says it means the purest and best of the fire. An-Nawawi says that smokeless fire is the flames mixed with the blackness of fire.

The Messenger, may Allah bless him and grant him peace, also reported that the jinn were created from fire when he said, 'The angels were created from light and the jinn were created from smokeless fire and Adam was created from what has been described to you.' *(Muslim transmits it.)*

But someone might ask: Allah informs us that the jinn are created from fire and also informs us that the flames harm and burn them but how can fire burn fire? The answer to that is that Allah has related the shaytans and jinn to fire in the same way that man is related to earth, clay and mud. What is meant by that in respect of man is that his origin is mud, not that he actually is mud. In the same way the jinn are fire in their origin.

The proof of that is in the hadith which Imam Ahmad b. Hanbal relates from Abu Sa'id al-Khudri: 'The Messenger of Allah, may Allah bless him and grant him peace, got up to pray the Morning Prayer and I was praying behind him. He recited and he became confused in the recitation. When he finished the prayer, he said, "If you could have only seen me grabbing Iblis and how I kept on throttling him until I felt the coolness of his spittle between my thumb and index finger. If it had not been for the supplication of my brother Sulayman, morning would have found him tied to one of the pillars of the mosque so that the children of Madina could have played with him. Whoever can avoid it should not let anyone come between him and the qibla." '

How can the spittle of someone made of burning fire be cold? If the jinn were still possessed of their fiery nature they would not have spittle.

Another indication that the jinn no longer possess their fiery nature is in the words of the Prophet, may Allah bless him and grant him peace, 'The enemy of Allah, Iblis, brought a brand of fire to put in my face.' *(An- Nasa'i relates this hadith from Abu'd-Darda' in the Chapter on Cursing Iblis and Seeking Refuge from him with Allah in the Prayer.)*

Imam Ahmad relates that a man asked 'Abdu'r-Rahman b. Khanbash what the Messenger of Allah, may Allah bless him and grant him peace, did when the shaytans meant to harm him. 'Abdu'r-Rahman said that some shaytans came down on the Messenger of Allah, may Allah bless him and grant him peace, from the valleys and canyons, including a shaytan with a fire-brand with which he wanted to burn the Messenger of Allah, may Allah bless him and grant him peace. 'Abdu'r-Rahman said that the Prophet was alarmed and Ja'far said that he had no doubt that he would be. 'Abdu'r-Rahman continued, 'He began to hesitate and Jibril, peace be upon him, came and said, "Muhammad, speak!"

'He replied, "What shall I say?"

'Jibril said, "Say: I seek refuge with the perfect words of Allah, which neither the pious nor impious overstep, and from the evil of what He created, and from the evil of what descends from the sky and from the evil that rises in it, and from the evil of what is sown in the land and from the evil of what comes out of it, and from the evil of the temptations of night and day, and from the evil of every visitor except a visitor who brings good, O Merciful One!" ' The fire of the shaytans was extinguished and Allah defeated them.

This evidence makes it clear that if the jinn had retained their fiery nature and were burning fire, the 'ifrits or shaytans among them would not have needed to carry a fire-brand. Since the hand of a shaytan or 'ifrit or any of their limbs do not burn man when they touch him, as real fire burns man by touch, that would indicate that the fire is submerged in the other elements so that the limbs or things that come from the body like spittle are cold in the way such things usually are, as the Prophet, may Allah bless him and grant him peace, said, 'until I felt the coolness of his spittle.'

There is no doubt that they eat and drink from what we eat and drink and that this gives their bodies sustenance and growth according to the nature of the food - hot and cold, wet and dry. This is in addition to how they are propagated from the fiery element which has become one of the four humours in their make up.[1]

WHEN WERE THE JINN CREATED?

The jinn were created before man was created. Allah says,

'We created man from dried clay from black mud
and We created the jinn before
from the fire of hot wind.' (15:26-27)

Allah makes it clear in this ayat that the jinn were created before man.

THE TYPES OF JINN

There are three types of jinn as stated in the hadith of the Prophet, may Allah bless him and grant him peace, in which he says, 'There are three types of jinn. One type flies through the air. Another type consists of snakes and dogs. A third is based in one place but travels about.' *(Al-Hakam and at-Tabarani transmit it and al-Bayhaqi also transmits it in* Names and Attributes *with a sound isnad.)*

Abu'd-Darda' said that the Messenger of Allah, may Allah bless him and grant him peace, said, 'Allah created three types of jinn. One type are snakes and scorpions and creeping things of the earth. One type is like the wind in the air. Another type are subject to reckoning and punishment.'

DO THE JINN HAVE BODIES?

Those who acknowledge the existence of the jinn disagree on this point and there are two positions about it. One group say that the jinn do not have bodies of their own nor do they inhabit bodies and that they exist independently.

The other group say that the jinn do have bodies, but those who

[1] i.e. hot, cold, wet and dry.

say this have a further disagreement. Some say that they have definite bodies and personal forms and that it is quite possible that these bodies have some density.

Others say that their bodies are so subtle that our eyes are too weak to see them. That is the only reason we cannot see them. If Allah were to strengthen our eyes or make their bodies denser, we would see them. The fineness of their physical forms is indicated by what Allah says,

'Surely he (Shaytan) sees you, he and his tribe, from where you see them not.' (7:27)

If we could see them with no barrier from behind which they whisper to us and they were dense, then we would be able to see them as they see us and as they see each other. The fact that in our world both our state and their state is different from that indicates the soundness of what we have said.

These are some of the opinions which seek to explain the nature of the bodies of the jinn. We must take note of the fact, however, that knowing whether the bodies of the jinn are subtle or dense can only come from direct witnessing or a report coming from Allah or from the Messenger of Allah and neither exist. It is for that reason that we hesitate to make a statement on this matter.

DO THE JINN HAVE OTHER NAMES?

Yes, the jinn have a variety of names which have been given by the theologians and scholars of Arabic. We will mention some of them:

Jinni: used by the Arabs to refer to one particular jinn.

'Amir (Resident jinn): used to mean that he is one of those who live with people.

Shaytan: used for a jinni who is malicious and has become wicked.

'Ifrit: used for a jinni who is stronger and more powerful than a shaytan.

It might be asked why they are called 'jinn'. They are called jinn because of their being concealed (*ijtinan*) from sight as Allah says,

'Surely he sees you, he and his tribe, from where you see them not.' (7:27)

DO THE JINN HAVE THE POWER TO TAKE ON FORMS?

The jinn possess a great power to take on forms and change shape. They can take on the form of snakes and scorpions, the form of horses, cattle, camels and sheep, and the form of birds. Indeed, they have the power to appear in human form. Reports have come which confirm this.

It is reported that Shaytan took on the form of an old man of Najd when the Quraysh gathered in the Dar al-Nadwa to discuss the Messenger, may Allah bless him and grant him peace, and whether they should kill him, imprison him or expel him. Shaytan suggested to them that they should kill him.

Muslim relates from Abu Sa'id al-Khudri said the Messenger of Allah, may Allah bless him and grant him peace, said, 'A group of jinn in Madina has become Muslim. If one of you sees any of these resident jinn , he should issue it a warning for three days. Then if it appears to you after that kill it, for it is a shaytan.'

THE CAPABILITIES AND POWERS OF THE JINN

The jinn have powers and capabilities that are beyond man. One of them is their extraordinary power of movement. Perhaps the example of this which first comes to mind is the promise of the 'ifrit of the jinn to Sulayman to bring the throne of the Queen of Yemen to Jerusalem in less time than it took Sulayman to rise from his assembly.

'An 'ifrit of the jinn said,
"I will bring it to you before you rise from your place.
I have the strength for it and I am trusty." ' (27:39)

They also have the power to take on the form of human beings, animals, birds and other things.

They have the power to rise up to high places in the heaven and to eavesdrop on the reports of heaven. That was before Muhammad, may Allah bless him and grant him peace, was sent.

DO THE JINN DIE?

There is no doubt that the jinn do die since they fall under what Allah says,

**'All that dwells upon the earth perishes,
yet still abides the Face of Your Lord, majestic, splendid.
So which of your Lord's bounties will you two deny?' (55:26-28)**

The Prophet, may Allah bless him and grant him peace, said in his prayer, 'I seek refuge in Your might. There is no god but You, O You who do not die! The jinn and men die.' *(Al-Bukhari relates it.)*

As for how long they live, our only knowledge about that is what Allah tells us concerning Iblis, that he will be watching and waiting until the Day of Rising.

**'He said, "Respite me until the day they shall be raised."
He said, "You are among those who are respited." ' (7:14-15)**

This ayat indicates that there are others who are respited in addition to Iblis. The Qur'an does not indicate, however, that all the jinn are respited, so while it is possible that some of the jinn will be respited, there is no indication that all of them are.

There are reports which indicate that they do die. One of them is Khalid ibn al-Walid's killing of the shaytan, al-'Uzza (the tree which the Arabs worshipped in the Time of Ignorance). There is also the Companion who killed a jinn that had taken the form of a viper and other such reports.

There is a clear statement about this by Ibn 'Abbas saying that it is Iblis alone who has been given the respite.

HOW DOES SHAYTAN WALK?

The Messenger of Allah, may Allah bless him and grant him peace, said, 'None of you should walk with just one sandal. Shaytan walks with one sandal.' (*Muslim, Abu Da'ud, at-Tirmidhi and Ibn Majah all mention it.*)

He also said, 'When one of you breaks his sandal-strap, he should not walk in the other one until he mends it.' (*Muslim relates it from Abu Hurayra in the Book of Dress and Adornment.*)

WHAT IS THE TIME WHEN SHAYTAN IS MOST FREQUENTLY PRESENT?

Shaytan is most frequently present at nightfall. It is established that the Messenger of Allah, may Allah bless him and grant him peace, said, 'As night comes in and it is dusk, then keep your children in for shaytans gather at that time. When an hour of the time goes by, then let them out. Close the doors and mention the name of Allah. Shaytan does not open a closed door.' (*Al-Bukhari relates it from Jabir b. 'Abdullah.*)

WHERE IS THE THRONE OF IBLIS?

The throne of Iblis is on the sea. Imam Ahmad b. Hanbal relates that Jabir said that the Messenger of Allah, may Allah bless him and grant him peace, said, 'Iblis places his throne on the sea. Then he sends forth his armies. The nearest of them to him in rank is the greatest in sedition. One of them comes and says, "I did such-and-such." He says, "You did not do anything." Then another comes and says, "I did not leave him until I had split him from his wife." He brings him near - or clasps him - and says, "You did well." '

THE ACTIONS WHICH IBLIS DID BEFORE THE SONS OF ADAM

Al-Baghawi mentions that Iblis was the first to wail.

Al-Hasan al-Basri said that Iblis made analogies and the sun and moon were worshipped by way of analogies.

This means that Iblis looked at himself and made a comparison between himself and Adam and thought that he was nobler than Adam. Therefore he refused to prostrate although he and all the angels had been commanded to do so.

Jabir related in a *marfu'* hadith that he was the first to sing.

Ibn Abi Shayba related that Maymun b. Mahran said, 'I asked Ibn 'Umar, "Who was the first to call 'Isha' (evening) *'Utama'* (darkness)?" He replied, "Shaytan." '

IS IBLIS A JINN OR AN ANGEL?

There are contrary and divergent opinions on this matter. Imam Hasan al- Banna confirms in his book *In the Shade of the Qur'an*, that he is one of the jinn when he says in commenting on what Allah has said, 'except Iblis'. 'The context reveals that Iblis was not one of the angels though he was with them. If he had been one of them, he would not have rebelled. Their primary quality is that "they do not rebel against Allah in what He commands them and they do as they are commanded." The word "except" here does not show that he was one of them. The fact that he was with them allows this exception to be used. Iblis was one of the jinn according to the text of the Qur'an. Allah created the jinn from smokeless fire. This is a clear statement that he was not one of the angels.'

Certain people from both previous and modern times have disagreed about this point. They use as their proof the words of Allah,

'When We said to the angels, "Prostrate to Adam,"
they prostrated except for Iblis.
He refused and was arrogant
and was one of the unbelievers.' (2:34)

and other examples in which Allah excepts Iblis from the angels. One only makes an exception, they say, from something which is of the same kind; and that the books of Qur'anic commentary and history have transmitted to us statements from a group of scholars who mention that Iblis was one of the angels. These scholars say that he was a guardian of the Garden or the lower heaven and that he was one of the noblest of the angels and from the noblest tribe among them, etc.

Ibn Kathir, however, points out that the early scholars related many traditions about this point. Most of them came from Jewish sources which were quoted so that they could be investigated. Allah has the best knowledge of the standing of many of them. Some of them are most definitely lies since they are contrary to the truth which we possess.

The proof that they put forward to us, namely that Allah excepted Iblis from the angels, is not an absolute proof because the possibility remains that the exception is disconnected. Indeed, that is the truth because of Allah's statement that he is one of the jinn,

'Iblis was one of the jinn
and deviated from the command of his Lord.' (18:50)

One of the proofs that Iblis was one of the jinn is that Iblis said about himself to the Lord of Might,

'You created me from fire
and You created him from clay.' (7:12)

There is also the fact that Iblis has offspring in contrast to the angels who do not.

Furthermore, as Allah mentions, the angels

'. . . do not rebel in what Allah has commanded them and do what they are commanded.' (66:6)

Also, the angels are created from light and the jinn are created from fire. The Messenger of Allah, may Allah bless him and grant him peace, said, 'The angels were created from light and the jinn were created from smokeless fire and Adam was created from what has been described to you,' *(Muslim relates this from 'A'isha.)*

DO THE JINN FEEL ENVY? CAN THEY HARM US?

Yes. There are two sorts of evil eye – human and that of the jinn.

There is a sound hadith from Umm Salama, may Allah be pleased with her, that the Prophet, may Allah bless him and grant him peace, saw a slavegirl in her house with yellowness in her face. He said, 'Use a spell for her. She has been afflicted by the evil eye.' (*Al-Bukhari relates it in the Book of Medicine.*)

Al-Husayn b. Mas'ud al-Farra' says that 'yellowness' means the influence of the evil eye, i.e. from the jinn.

Al-Bukhari relates from Abu Hurayra that the Prophet, may Allah bless him and grant him peace, said, 'The evil eye is real and the prophets forbade tattooing.'

CHAPTER TWO

THE OBLIGATIONS OF THE JINN

Comprising:

The obligations of the jinn.
Are there messengers and prophets among the jinn?
The universal mission of the Prophet to jinn and men.
Religions and sects among the jinn.
Are the jinn rewarded for their actions?

THE OBLIGATIONS OF THE JINN

Muslim thinkers all agree that the jinn are responsible for their actions. As proof of this, they cite the instances where the Qur'an censures and curses the jinn and mentions the punishment that Allah has prepared for them. Allah - glory be to Him! - only treats in this way those who oppose the command and prohibition, commit grave wrong actions, and violate things which are forbidden when they are capable of choice and discrimination.

Ibn Muflah says in his book *Al-Furu'*, 'In principle, the jinn are responsible for their actions. Those of them who disbelieve will enter the Fire and those of them who believe will enter the Garden according to Malik and ash-Shafi'i, may Allah be pleased with them. They do not become dust like the animals, and the reward of those of them who believe is that they are saved from the Fire. This is contrary to the opinion of Abu Hanifa and al-Layth b. Sa'd and those who share their opinion. The apparent meaning of the first position is that the jinn are in the Garden just as others are, commensurate with their reward, contrary to those like Mujahid who say that they neither eat nor drink in it or, like 'Umar ibn 'Abdu'l-'Aziz, that they are on the outskirts of the Garden. Ibn Hamid said in his book *Lawami' al-Anwar*, "The jinn are the same as men regarding obligation and acts of worship." ' (Vol. 2, p. 222)

The obligations of the jinn are not the same as the obligations of men. Their obligations are according to their nature and their conditions. Ibn Taimiyya says in *Majmu' al-Fatawa*, [4:233], 'The jinn are commanded to observe the roots and branches appropriate to them. They are different from mankind in constitution and experience, so what they are commanded and forbidden is different from what applies to men. However, they are similar to mankind in being bound by the commands and prohibitions, the halal and the haram. I do not know of any dispute regarding this among the Muslims.'

ARE THERE MESSENGERS AND PROPHETS AMONG THE JINN?

Ad-Dahhak was asked whether the jinn had a prophet before the Prophet Muhammad, may Allah bless him and grant him peace, was sent. He said, 'Have you not heard Allah's words,

**"Company of jinn and men,
did not messengers come to you from among you?..." (6:130)**

Ad-Dahhak was of the opinion that this ayat indicates that Allah has sent messengers from among the jinn.

However, in answer to this, the ayat does not clearly state that these messengers were jinn or men because the words, 'from among you' could equally apply to either group. It could mean messengers from each of them and it could mean messengers from men and jinn as one group. It has been verified for one group, namely men.

There is disagreement about this among scholars and there are two positions. The majority of both ancient and modern scholars believe that there has never been any messenger from the jinn and that messengers only come from among mankind. A minority of scholars say that the jinn do have messengers. Ad-Dahhak is among those who hold this position as has already been mentioned, and Ibn al-Jawzi says that it is the apparent meaning of what the Qur'an says.

THE UNIVERSAL MISSION OF THE PROPHET TO JINN AND MEN

Muslim scholars agree that Muhammad, may Allah bless him and grant him peace, was sent by Allah - glory be to Him! - to all jinn and men.

The Companions, the Followers, the Imams of the Muslims and all Muslim groups (*Ahl as-Sunna wa'l-Jama'at*) agree on this basic principle as stated by Ibn Taimiyya - may Allah be pleased with all of them.

The challenge of the Qur'an to jinn and men indicates this,

**'Say: If jinn and men banded together
to produce the like of this Qur'an,
they would never produce its like,
not even if they backed each other.' (17:88)**

A group of the jinn were quickly moved to believe when they heard the Qur'an.

'Say: it has been revealed to me

that a company of the jinn gave ear.
Then they said, "We have indeed heard
a wonderful Qur'an, guiding to right action.
We believe in it,
and we will not associate anyone with our Lord." ' (72:1-2)

Allah, glory be to Him!, mentions this group who heard the Qur'an and believed in it in Sura Al-Ahqaf,

'And when We turned to you
a company of jinn who wished to hear the Qur'an,
and when they were in its presence
they said, "Be silent!"
Then, when it was finished,
they turned back to their people, warning.
They said, "Our people, we have heard a Book
that was sent down after Musa,
confirming what was before it,
guiding to the truth and to a straight path.
O our people, answer Allah's summoner
and believe in Him
and He will forgive you some of your wrong actions,
and protect you from a painful punishment.
Whosoever answers not Allah's summoner
cannot frustrate Allah in the earth
and he has no protectors apart from Him,
those are in clear misguidance." ' (46:29-32)

These Qur'anic ayats indicate the absolute proof of the universality of the message of the Prophet to men and jinn.

As for the hadiths which indicate this, one of them which is confirmed in the two Sahih volumes is the hadith of Jabir b. 'Abdullah in which the Messenger of Allah, may Allah bless him and grant him peace, mentioned that he had been given five things that no other prophet before him had been given, and among them was that the Prophets were sent to their own peoples and he was sent to all people.

Al-Jawhari comments that 'people' consists of men and jinn, whilst ar-Raghib says that 'people' consists of every living thing with the capacity for reflection. The jinn possess reflection. The word 'people' (*nas*) comes from the verb, *nasa*, meaning to move to and fro.

Therefore Muhammad is the Messenger of Allah to men and jinn, a warner and a bringer of good news. (That is something in which he has been preferred over all the other prophets.)

RELIGIONS AND SECTS AMONG THE JINN

Allah tells us that the jinn said,

'Some of us are righteous, and some of us are otherwise: we are parties differing.' (72:11)

'Some of us have surrendered and some of us have deviated. Those who have surrendered sought right guidance. As for those who have deviated, they have become firewood for Jahannam.' (72:14-15)

The jinn have different schools. As-Suddi said, 'The jinn are like you. They have Murji'ites, Qadiris, Rafidites and Kharijites.[1] *

ARE THE JINN REWARDED FOR THEIR ACTIONS?

The scholars have two opinions on this matter. One group say that the jinn are rewarded for obedience and punished for rebellion. Malik, Ibn Abi Layla, ash-Shafi'i, Ahmad b. Hanbal, and Ibn 'Abbas are amongst those who take this position.

The second group say that their only reward is to be saved from the Fire. Then they will be told, 'Be dust like the animals.' This is the position of Abu Hanifa and Layth b. Abi Salim amongst others.

The preferable position is that the jinn are rewarded and punished. The Qur'an indicates this when Allah says,

'All have degrees according to what they have done...' (6:132)

'. . . Against them has been realized the Word concerning nations that passed away before them, men and jinn alike.' (41:25)

'Some of us have surrendered and some of us have deviated. Those who have surrendered sought right guidance. As for those who have deviated, they have become firewood for Jahannam.' (72:14-15)

* See Glossary

One of the clearest proofs of this is found in the words of Allah,

'For such as fear the Station of his Lord,
for them shall be two gardens -
O which of your Lord's bounties will you two deny?'
(55:46-47)

and so on to the end of the sura.

Both men and jinn are addressed. Allah - glory be to Him! - bestows on them the reward of the Garden and describes it for them and makes them yearn for it. This indicates that they will receive what He has bestowed on them if they believe.

There is also a hadith to the effect that the Messenger of Allah, may Allah bless him and grant him peace, said to his Companions when he was reciting this sura to them, 'The jinn had a better answer and response than you. Whenever an ayat was recited to them, they said, "We do not deny any of Your blessings, O our Lord!" ' (*At-Tirmidhi transmits it.*)

This makes sense because Allah has threatened those of them who reject and rebel with the Fire. How, therefore, can those of them who do obey not enter the Garden when Allah, glory be to Him!, is the Wise, the Just?

We must take note of the fact that, in spite of scholars disagreeing about whether the believing jinn will be punished in the Next World, Allah mentions in His Immense Book,

'The Fire will be a lodging for them.' (41:24)

and he says,

'As for those who have deviated,
they have become firewood for Jahannam.' (72:15)

CHAPTER THREE

THE JINN IN THEIR OWN SPHERE

Comprising:

Do they marry and have children?
Can jinn and men inter-marry?
Do the jinn eat and drink?
The homes and haunts of the jinn.
The animals of the jinn.

DO THEY MARRY AND HAVE CHILDREN?

Yes, the jinn marry and have children. This fact is indicated in the Book and Sunna.

In the Book, Allah says,

'What, do you take him and his offspring to be your friends, apart from Me, when they are an enemy to you?' (18:50)

This ayat indicates that they marry for the sake of offspring. Qadi 'Abdu'l- Jabbar said, 'Offspring refers to children and family.' The fact that they are subtle creatures does not prevent them from reproducing. Many organisms only become visible by minute observation because they are so fine. That does not prevent them from reproducing since what they reproduce is also fine.

Allah says,

'Untouched before by any man or jinn.' (55:56)

This ayat indicates that they have intercourse. This refers to deflowering or intercourse in general.

As for the sunna, the Messenger of Allah, may Allah bless him and grant him peace, said, 'The jinn reproduce as the children of Adam reproduce. But there are more of them.' (*Ibn Abi Hatim and Abu'sh-Shaykh relate it from Qatada in* Al-'Udhma'.)

CAN JINN AND MEN INTER-MARRY?

It is common belief in certain quarters that a man may marry a jinn woman or that a human woman may marry or become engaged to a jinn man. How true is this statement?

Marriage between men and jinn can take place for Allah says,

'...Share with them in their wealth and children...' (17:64)

The Messenger of Allah, may Allah bless him and grant him peace, said, 'When a man has intercourse with his wife and does not say, "In the name of Allah," Shaytan folds himself up in his urethra and has intercourse along with him.' (*Ash-Shibli mentions it in* Akam al-Marjan.)

Ibn Jarir relates that Ibn 'Abbas said, 'When a man goes to his wife while she is menstruating, Shaytan precedes him. She conceives and brings forth an effete one (*mukhannath*). These effete ones are the children of the jinn.'

Ash-Shibli relates from Qadi Jalalu'd-din ar-Razi that his father told about how he went on a journey to fetch his family from the east:

'After we had passed Ilbira, the rain forced us to seek shelter, so we went to sleep in a cave. There was a group of us. While I was asleep, something awakened me. I woke up and there was a woman surrounded by some other women. She had one eye fixed open. I was alarmed. She said, "Don't be afraid. I have come to marry you to one of my daughters who is like the moon." I replied out of my fear of her, "By the choice of Allah." I looked again and some men had appeared. They looked like the woman who had come to me with their eyes fixed open. They appeared to be a Qadi and witnesses. The Qadi performed the engagement and marriage contract and I accepted. Then they got up. The woman returned with a beautiful girl whose eye, however, was like that of her mother. She left her with me and departed.

'My fear and distaste increased. I began to throw stones at the people about me so as to wake them up. When one of them finally woke up, I began to offer supplications. Then it was time to depart and we set off. The young girl did not leave me. This state of things went on for three days. On the fourth day, the woman came to me and said, "It seems that you do not like this young girl and want to part from her." I said, "Yes, by Allah!" She said, "You have divorced her." Then she left and I did not see her again.'

Despite the great number of reports that indicate that intercourse between men and jinn does take place, some people maintain that since jinn are from the element of fire and man is from the four elements (air, water, earth, and fire), the element of fire prevents human sperm from being in the womb of a female jinn since sperm is wet and the fiery heat is too intense for it.

The answer to this objection is that the jinn were created from fire, but they no longer have their fiery nature. They have been transformed from it by eating, drinking, procreation, and reproduction, just as the sons of Adam have been transformed from their earthy element in the same way.

Furthermore, the one who was created from fire was the father of the jinn in the way that Adam, the father of men, was created from earth. As far as all the other jinn are concerned, other than their forefather, they are not created from actual fire just as none of the children of Adam are created from actual earth.

Moreover, the Prophet said that he felt on his hand the 'coolness' of the spittle of the shaytan who appeared to him while he was praying and whom he throttled, as we have already mentioned.

This saliva of Shaytan which the Prophet, may Allah bless him and grant him peace, refers to is a proof that he has changed from his fiery element. If he had retained that state then where did this coldness come from?

DO THE JINN EAT AND DRINK?

There are three positions regarding the jinn eating and drinking, and a fourth sub-branch.

The first is that none of the jinn eat or drink.

The second is that one kind of them do not eat or drink and another kind do eat and drink.

The third is that all the jinn eat and drink.

Those who take this last position disagree about how they eat and drink. Some say that their eating and drinking consists of sniffing and inhaling, not chewing and swallowing. This position is not supported by any proof. Others say that their eating and drinking consists of chewing and swallowing. This statement is testified to in sound hadith and clear widespread reports.

The fact that they chew and swallow is indicated by the hadith of Umayya b. Makhshi transmitted by Abu Da'ud. It says, 'Shaytan continued to eat with him. When he mentioned the name of Allah, the Mighty and Majestic, he vomited what was in his belly.'

In the *Sahih* of al-Bukhari in a hadith related by Abu Hurayra, the Prophet, may Allah bless him and grant him peace, commanded him to bring him some stones with which to clean himself. He said, 'Do not bring bones or dung.' When Abu Hurayra asked the Messenger later on about the reason for his forbidding bones and dung, he said, 'They are part of the food of the jinn. A delegation of the Nasibi jinn, and they are the best of the jinn, came to me and asked me for provision. I prayed to Allah for them that they would not pass by a bone or a piece of dung without finding some food from it.'

In the *Sunan* of at-Tirmidhi, it says in a transmission with a sound isnad, 'Do not clean yourself with bones or dung. They are the provision of your brothers among the jinn.'

The Prophet, may Allah bless him and grant him peace, informed us that Shaytan eats with his left hand and he commanded us to do the opposite of that. Imam Muslim transmits from Ibn 'Umar that the Prophet said, 'When one of you eats, he should eat with his right hand. When he drinks, he should drink with his right hand. Shaytan eats with his left hand and drinks with his left hand.'

These hadiths are proof that the shaytans eat and drink. Some people have taken this last hadith and ones like it as being metaphorical, saying that the Prophet's words, 'Shaytan eats with his left hand' means that eating with the left hand is a form of eating which appeals to Shaytan in the same way that he indicated that rouge was 'the adornment of Shaytan' meaning that Shaytan makes rouge seem attractive and arouses the desire to use to it. Similarly, Shaytan urges people to eat with the left hand and drink with the left hand and makes it seem attractive. Some scholars have said that this point amounts to nothing as there is no object in taking words metaphorically when it is possible that they are in any way real and literal.'

THE HOMES AND HAUNTS OF THE JINN

The jinn live all over the earth, although they are found mostly in deserts, ruins, and places of impurity like dunghills, bathrooms, and graveyards.

That is why the shaykhs to whom the shaytans had links went to many such places which are their haunts.

There are hadiths of the Prophet which forbid us to pray in the bathroom because there is impurity there and because it is the haunt of shaytans, or in the graveyard because, as well as being a means of associating things with Allah, the graves are the haunts of shaytans.

They are frequently found in places where they can cause a lot of mischief and corruption, like markets. That is why the Prophet, may Allah bless him and grant him peace, gave some advice to one of the Companions, saying, 'If possible, do not be the first to enter the market nor the last to leave it. It is the battle-ground of Shaytan and he raises his banner there.' (*Muslim transmits it in the* Sahih.)

Shaytan also dwells in the houses of the children of Adam. Saying, 'In the name of Allah' expels him and drives him off. Muslim and Abu Da'ud relate from Jabir that the Messenger of Allah, may Allah bless him and grant him peace, said, 'When a man mentions the name of Allah on entering his house and when he eats, Shaytan says to his cohorts, "You have no place to spend the night and no supper." When the man mentions Allah on entering but does not mention Him when He eats, he says, "You have got supper but no place to spend the night." If he does not mention the name of Allah when he enters, Shaytan says, "You have got a place to spend the night and supper." '

Among the places where Shaytan likes to sit is 'between the sun and the shade.' That is why the Prophet, may Allah bless him and grant him peace, forbade people to sit there as has been related in the hadith which is transmitted in the *Sunan* collections.

THE ANIMALS OF THE JINN

The Prophet, may Allah bless him and grant him peace, mentioned that the jinn have animals. There is a sound hadith that Muslim relates from Ibn Mas'ud that when the jinn asked the Messenger for provision, he said, 'You have every bone over which the name of Allah has been mentioned which comes to your hands, more abundant than the meat that was on it. Every piece of dung is fodder for your beasts.'

In this hadith, the Prophet, may Allah bless him and grant him peace, indicates that the jinn have beasts and that the dung of the animals of men is fodder for their beasts.

CHAPTER FOUR

THE JINN AND KNOWLEDGE

Comprising:

The jinn's transmission of hadith.
Preachers among the jinn.
The jinn's knowledge of the types of wisdom.

THE JINN'S TRANSMISSION OF HADITH

It has come in certain traditions and reports that there are certain individuals among the jinn who transmit hadiths from the Messenger of Allah, may Allah bless him and grant him peace. We will mention some of these reports.

Ubayy b. Ka'b said, 'Some people set out for Makka and lost their way. When they were on the verge of death, they put on their shrouds and lay down to wait for death. A jinn came out to them from the trees and said, "I am the last of the group who listened to the Prophet, may Allah bless him and grant him peace. I heard him say, 'The believer is the brother of the believer. They can rely on each other's wells and guidance. Here is water and here is the path." Then he guided them to water and guided them to the road.' (*Abu Nu'aym transmits it.*)

The client of 'Abdu'r-Rahman b. Bishr said, 'Some people set out on hajj during the amirate of 'Uthman. They were overcome with thirst and came to some salty water. One of them advised pressing on for he feared that the water would kill them. "There is water ahead of you," he said, so they travelled on until evening and still did not find any water. They said to each other, "We should go back to the salty water." They set out at nightfall and reached an acacia tree. A man who was very black came out to greet them. "Caravan!" he said, "I heard the Messenger of Allah, may Allah bless him and grant him peace, say, 'Whoever believes in Allah and the Last Day should love for the Muslims what he loves for himself and should hate for the Muslims what he hates for himself.' Keep going until you reach a hill. Then go to the left of it and there is water there."

'One of them said, "By Allah, we think that it was a shaytan." Another said, "A shaytan would never speak in such a way as he spoke to you," meaning that he was a believing jinn.

'They went on until they reached the place he had described to them and found water.' (*Abu Bakr b. Muhammad transmits it.*)

PREACHERS AMONG THE JINN

As there are preachers among mankind, so there are also preachers among the jinn. Indeed, some of the preachers of the jinn possess many types of wisdom and excellent preaching. This might become clearer to you in the course of the following narration:

Abu Khalifa al-'Abdi said, 'A small son of mine died and I was very upset about him. I could not sleep. By Allah, that night I was in my room on my bed and no one else was in the room. I was thinking about my son when someone called to me from a corner of the room, "Peace be upon you and the mercy of Allah, Khalifa!" I replied, "And peace be upon you and the mercy of Allah."

'I was very alarmed and recited some ayats from the end of Sura Ali 'Imran until I reached the words of Allah,

"What is with Allah is better for the pious." (3:197)

'Then he said, "O Abu Khalifa!" I replied, "At your service."

'He said, "Why do you want your son in particular to live rather than people in general? Who is more noble in the eyes of Allah - you or Muhammad? His son Ibrahim died and he said, 'The eyes weep and the heart is sad, but we do not say what will anger the Lord.' Or do you want to avert death from your son while it is written for all creatures? Do you intend to be angry with Allah and oppose His management of His creation? By Allah, if it had not been for death, the earth would not be wide enough for them! If it were not for grief, creatures would not benefit from life!"

'Then he asked, "Do you need anything?" I said, "Who are you, may Allah have mercy on you?" He said, "A man from your neighbours among the jinn." ' (*Ibn Abi'd-Dunya transmits it.*)

THE JINN'S KNOWLEDGE OF THE TYPES OF WISDOM

Ishaq b. 'Ubaydullah b. Abi Firwa reported that a group of jinn took human form and came to a man and said, 'What thing would you most like to have?' He replied, 'Camels.' They said, 'You love wretchedness, worry, and long affliction. You will be exiled and far from those you love.'

Then they left him and went to someone else. They asked, 'What thing would you most like to have?' The man replied, 'Slaves.' They said, 'Useful might, anger like pins, property and cursing.'

They left him and went to someone else. They said, 'What thing would you most like to have?' He replied, 'I like sheep.' They said, 'Food for the one who eats and a gift to the asker. It will not bear you in war nor join you in the plunder nor rescue you from trouble.'

They left him and went to someone else. They said, 'What thing would you most like to have?' He replied, 'I like fields.' They said,

'Half of livelihood when they are tilled. When they are not tilled, they do not exist.'

They left him and went to someone else. They said, 'What thing would you most like to have?' He replied, 'How many of you are there so that I can offer you my hospitality?' He brought them bread and they said, 'Wheat is good.' Then he brought them meat and they said, 'A soul eating a soul. A little of it is better than a lot.' He brought them dates and milk. They said, 'The fruit of palm trees and the milk of cows. Eat in the name of Allah.' They ate.

They said, 'Tell us what the sharpest thing is. What the best thing is? What the most fragrant thing is?' He said, 'The sharpest thing is a sharp tooth feeding food into an empty stomach. The best thing is a morning cloud following an evening cloud over earth which is fruitful. The most fragrant thing is the sweet fragrance of flowers after rain.'

They said, 'Tell us what you would most like to have.' He replied, 'I would like death.' They said, 'You have desired something which no one before you has desired.' He said, 'Why not? If I am good, it safeguards my good action for me. If I am bad, it protects me from my evil. If I am rich, it guarantees my poverty. If I am poor, it safeguards my poverty for me.'

They said, 'Advise us and give us provision.' He brought them a skin of milk and said, 'This is your provision.' They said, 'Advise us.' He said, 'Say, "There is no god but Allah." That will be enough for you in what is before you and what is behind you.' They left him and thought him the best of jinn and men! (*Ibn Abi'd-Dunya transmits it.*)

CHAPTER FIVE

THE JINN AND THE PROPHETS

Comprising:

Shaytan in the ship of Nuh.
Shaytan and Musa.
Shaytan and 'Isa.
Can Shaytan take on the form of the Prophet?
The jinn reporting about the mission of the Prophet.

SHAYTAN IN THE SHIP OF NUH

'It says in the *Tablis Iblis*, 'When Nuh, peace be upon him, embarked on the ship, he saw an old man whom he did not recognise. Nuh said to him, "How have you come on board?" He replied, "I have come on in order to afflict the hearts of your companions so that their hearts will be with me and their bodies with you." Nuh, peace be upon him, said, "Get away, enemy of Allah!" Iblis said, "There are five things by which people are destroyed. I will tell you three of them and not tell you the other two." Allah, the Mighty and Blessed, revealed to Nuh, peace be upon him, "There is no need for the three. Command him to tell you about the two." He said, "People are destroyed by those two which are envy and avarice. Envy was cursed and became an accursed shaytan. Adam was allowed the entire Garden but because of avarice I got what I needed from him and he was expelled from the Garden." '

SHAYTAN AND MUSA

It says in the *Tablis Iblis*, 'Iblis met Musa and said, "Musa, Allah has chosen you for His message and spoken to you directly. I am one of Allah's creatures. I have done wrong and want to repent, so intercede with your Lord, the Mighty and Majestic, so that He will turn to me." Musa called on his Lord and was told, "Musa, your request has been granted." Musa met Iblis and told him, "You have been commanded to prostrate at the grave of Adam and He will turn to you." He was arrogant and became angry and said, "I did not prostrate to him while he was alive, how should I then prostrate to him now he is dead?!"

Then Iblis said, "Musa, you have a right of intercession with your Lord. Remember me on three occasions when I am not destroyed:

' "Remember me when you are angry. I move in your heart and my eye is in your eye and I flow in you as blood flows.

' "Remember me when you meet the enemy face to face. I come to the son of Adam when he meets the enemy face to face and remind him of his children, his wife and his family until he turns his back.

‘“Beware of sitting with a woman to whom you are not related. I am her messenger to you and your messenger to her.”’

SHAYTAN AND ‘ISA

Makhul Abu ‘Uthman said that once when ‘Isa, peace be upon him, was praying at the top of a mountain, Iblis came to him and said, ‘Don’t you believe in the determination and the decree?’ ‘Isa said, ‘Indeed I do.’ So he said to ‘Isa, ‘Then throw yourself over the edge and only what Allah has decreed for you will befall you.’ ‘Isa retorted, ‘The Lord puts His slave to the test and tries him. It is not proper for the slave to test his Lord.’ (*Ibn Abi’d-Dunya transmits it.*)

CAN SHAYTAN TAKE ON THE FORM OF THE PROPHET?

Shaytan does not take on the form of the Prophet, may Allah bless him and grant him peace, since the Prophet has said, ‘Whoever sees me in a dream has truly seen me. Shaytan does not take on my form.’ (*Muslim and al-Bukhari transmit it.*)

Since he cannot take on the form of the Prophet, may Allah bless him and grant him peace, it is even more fitting that he cannot take on the form of Allah, the Mighty and Exalted, and more likely that the vision of Allah the Mighty in a dream be true and that there not be any mixture in it from Shaytan. This is the position taken up by Abu Bakr b. al-‘Arabi amongst others.

Another group of scholars believe that the protection which makes it impossible for Shaytan to take on form and resemblance is only relevant to the Prophet, may Allah bless him and grant him peace, because he was a mortal whose form can be taken, and so Allah, the Mighty and Exalted, keeps Shaytan from taking on his form so that the vision of the Prophet does not become muddled with the false dream. The most seemly position is that it is not possible for Allah to have a form and so it is not possible for Shaytan to take on His form for Allah says of Himself, ‘There is nothing like Him. He is the Hearing, the Seeing.’

THE JINN REPORTING ABOUT THE MISSION OF THE PROPHET

Ahmad b. Hanbal transmits the following from Mujahid, 'While we were on the raid of Rawdas, an old man called Ibn 'Isa who had been alive in the Time of Ignorance told us, "I was herding a cow for some of our family when I heard a voice coming from within it, 'O such a wind! O eloquent words of a man who says, "There is no god but Allah"!' We went ahead to Makka and found that the Prophet, may Allah bless him and grant him peace, had left Makka." '

'Abdullah b. Ahmad said that the hadith is *gharib* (unusual) but with an excellent *isnad*. (*Ash-Shibli mentions it in* Akam al-Marjan.)
report to come to Madina about the Prophet, may Allah bless him and grant him peace, was to a certain woman from the people of Madina who had a jinn who followed her around. He would appear in the form of a bird and alight on the wall of her house. The woman said to him, 'Speak and tell us your news.' He said, 'A prophet has been sent in Makka who has forbidden some of us to stay and he has forbidden us fornication.'

CHAPTER SIX

MISCELLANY

Is it permitted to ask the jinn about the past and future?
The fettering of the rebellious jinn in Ramadan.
Are there some people who worship jinn?
Why do the jinn and shaytans obey charms and talismans?
The jinn's testifying for the mu'adhdhin on the Day of Rising.
Does Shaytan oppose the people in the mosque?
Do animals see Shaytan?

IS IT PERMITTED TO ASK THE JINN ABOUT THE PAST AND FUTURE?

Something about which there is no in doubt is that Allah has given the jinn the power to traverse great distances in a short time. This is proven by Allah's words,

'An 'Ifrit of the jinn said,
"I will bring it to you
before you rise from your place.' (27:39)

If someone asks a jinn about an event which has occurred or about someone in a distant land, it is possible that he has knowledge to impart about the event or the person's situation. It is also possible that he does not have any knowledge, goes to find out about it, returns and tells what he knows. All the same, it is only a single report and is only useful as opinion from which one cannot draw any conclusions other than background information.

As for asking the jinn about things which have not yet happened and believing them, based on the fact that they know the unseen, that is disbelief. It is established in the *Sahih* from Mu'awiya b. al-Hakam that when the Prophet, may Allah bless him and grant him peace, was asked about consulting soothsayers, he said, 'Do not go to them.' In the *Sahih* of Muslim, the Messenger of Allah, may Allah bless him and grant him peace, is reported as saying, 'The prayer of someone who goes to consult a diviner (*'arraf*) will not be accepted for forty days.'[1]

We must point out that if someone asks a person in order to test his state or to test what the *'arraf* conceals and he possesses the information to distinguish the true from the false, then that is permitted.

THE FETTERING OF THE REBELLIOUS JINN IN RAMADAN

Muslim transmits in a *marfu'* hadith from Abu Hurayra, 'When Ramadan comes, the gates of the Garden are opened and the gates of the Fire are closed and the shaytans are fettered.'

[1] The *'arraf* is a type of diviner. Ibn al-Athir says that it is an astrologer or an astrologer who claims knowledge of the unseen which Allah has kept exclusively for himself.

'Abdullah b. Ahmad said, 'I asked my father about the hadith, "When Ramadan comes, the shaytans are fettered." He said, "Yes." I said, "But a man has whisperings in Ramadan and is brought down (by Shaytan)." He said, "That is how the hadith has come."

CERTAIN PEOPLE WORSHIPPING THE JINN

Some people used to worship a group of the jinn. Then some of the jinn became Muslim, but those people continued to worship them. Then Allah revealed,

'Those they call upon are themselves
seeking the means to come to their Lord,
which of them shall be nearer;
they hope for His mercy and fear His punishment...' (17:57)

(Ahmad b. Hanbal transmits this from Ibn Mas'ud and Shu'ayb relates it from Al-A'mash.)

WHY DO THE JINN AND SHAYTANS OBEY CHARMS AND TALISMANS?

The unbelieving jinn and the shaytans among them choose the path of misguidance, and of causing error and wrong actions. Iblis and his armies desire evil and plot with it and seek it out. Iblis said, 'Now, by Your might, I shall beguile them all together, excepting those of Your servants among them who are sincere.' (38:82-83)

Iblis also said, 'What do You think? This (i.e. man) whom You have honoured above me - if You defer me to the Day of Rising, I shall assuredly master his seed, save a few.' (17:62)

If the nature or temperament of a man is corrupt, then he desires what will harm him and enjoys and loves it. Shaytan has a corrupt soul. When someone draws near him through charms, oaths, and books of spiritual magic that contain what he loves of disbelief and associating things with Allah, it is like a bribe to him, and therefore he carries out some of the man's desires.

The man with a foul soul begins to write down the words of Allah with something impure and he may reverse the letters of 'Say: He is Allah, One' (111:1) or the recitation of *Sura Ya Sin* or do other such things which please Shaytan. When someone says or writes what pleases the shaytans, then they in turn assist him in some of his desires - for instance, making a water source seep away or carrying him in the air to certain places or bringing him other people's property or by injuring someone he is hostile to.

THE JINN TESTIFYING FOR THE MU'ADHDHIN ON THE DAY OF RISING

The jinn will testify for the *mu'adhdhin* on the Day of Rising. The Sahih of al-Bukhari, the Muwatta', and other books have the hadith of Ibn Abi Sa'sa'a where Abu Sa'id al-Khudri says to him, 'I see that you love sheep and the desert. When you are out with your sheep or in the desert, call the prayer and raise your voice in the adhan because no jinn or man or anything within range hears the voice of the mu'adhdhin except that it bears witness for him on the Day of Rising.'

Abu Sa'id goes on to say, 'I heard the Messenger of Allah, may Allah bless him and grant him peace, say that.'

DOES SHAYTAN OPPOSE THE PEOPLE IN THE MOSQUE?

Yes. The Prophet of Allah, may Allah bless him and grant him peace, said, 'Make your rows straight, bring them near each other and stand shoulder to shoulder, for by the One in whose hand the soul of Muhammad is, I see Shaytan coming in through gaps in the row like small black sheep.' (*Abu Da'ud transmits it.*)

The Prophet, may Allah bless him and grant him peace, said, 'When one of you is in the mosque, Shaytan comes to him and breaks him as a man would break his riding animal. When he is tamed for him, he hobbles him or bridles him.' (*Ahmad b. Hanbal transmits it.*)

Abu Hurayra, who related the hadith, commented, 'You see that. If he is hobbled, you can see him lounging, not remembering Allah. If he is bridled, his mouth opens and he does not mention Allah the Mighty.'

DO ANIMALS SEE SHAYTAN?

Yes. There are animals which see Shaytan. The Messenger of Allah, may Allah bless him and grant him peace, said, 'When you hear the cock crowing, then ask Allah for His bounty for it has seen an angel. When you hear the braying of a donkey, then seek refuge in Allah from Shaytan for it has seen a shaytan.' (*Al-Bukhari transmits it from Abu Hurayra.*)

CHAPTER SEVEN

MANIFESTATIONS OF THE STRUGGLE BETWEEN SHAYTAN AND MAN

Comprising:

Causes of the enmity between Shaytan and man.
The reasons which led Iblis to fall into error.
What is the greatest goal of Shaytan?
The things to which Shaytan calls man.
What act of rebellion does Iblis prefer?
The jinn bringing down a man and its cure.
The jinn and the plague.
False menstruation is from Shaytan.
Shaytan and dreams.
The whispering of Shaytan.
Haste is from Shaytan.
Shaytan clings to the unjust judge.
Shaytan binding the head of the sleeper.
Shaytan's touching man.
Shaytan is present when a child is born.
Shaytan's presence during intercourse.
Shaytan's presence in all the affairs of man.

THE CAUSES OF THE ENMITY BETWEEN SHAYTAN AND MAN

The enmity between Shaytan and man goes back to the depths of the distant past when Allah created Adam and breathed into him of His spirit. Then Allah the Glorious commanded the angels to prostrate to Adam. Iblis was worshipping Allah with the angels, and so he was included in the command. But he refused and was haughty and was not one of those who prostrated. When Allah asked why he had refused to prostrate, he replied, 'I am better than him. You created me from fire and You created him from clay.' Here is the hidden reason for the enmity between Shaytan and man.

The best source that we can review for the history of the enmity between them is the Noble Qur'an. Allah describes the story of the conflict in full:

'We created you and then shaped you. Then We said to the angels, "Prostrate to Adam," so they prostrated except for Iblis. He was not one of those who prostrated.

'He said, "What kept you from prostrating when I commanded you?" He said, "I am better than him. You created me from fire and You created him from clay." He said, "Get down out of it. It is not for you to become haughty here, so get out. You are among the humbled." He said, "Respite me until the day that they will be raised." He said, "You are among those who are respited."

'He said, "Now, because You have sent me astray, I shall surely sit in ambush for them on Your straight path, then I shall come on them from before them and from behind them, from their right hands and their left hands. You will not find most of them thankful."

'He said, "Go out of it, despised and banished. Those of them that follow you - I shall assuredly fill Jahannam with all of them."

'O Adam, inherit, you and your wife, the Garden, and eat wherever you wish, but do not come near this tree, lest you be one of the wrongdoers.

'Then Shaytan whispered to them to reveal to them that which was hidden from them of their private parts. He said, "Your Lord has only prohibited you from this tree lest you become angels or lest you become immortals." And he swore to them, "Truly, I am a sincere adviser for you."

'So he led them on by delusion, and when they tasted of the tree, their private parts were revealed to them, so they took to stitching upon themselves leaves of the Garden. And their Lord called to them, "Did I not forbid you this tree and say to you, 'Shaytan is a clear enemy for you.' "

'They said, "Lord, we have wronged ourselves, and if You do not forgive us and have mercy on us, we shall surely be among the lost." He said, "Get down, each of you an enemy to one another. In the earth you shall have rest and enjoyment for a time." ' (7:11-24)

The most important thing to deduce from these ayats is to know that the enmity of Shaytan will not change or abate because he is convinced that his banishment, curse, and expulsion from the Garden was because of our father, Adam, and that he is bound to take revenge on Adam and his descendants after him. That is why the Qur'an goes on at some length to put us on our guard against Shaytan. Allah says, *'O children of Adam, do not let Shaytan tempt you...' (7:27)*

THE REASONS WHICH LED IBLIS TO FALL INTO ERROR

When Iblis said, 'I am better than him. You created me from fire and You created him from clay', he was mistaken for the following reasons:

1. Even though one obtains certain benefits and enjoyment from fire, evil is still concealed in it. Its evil is only averted by subduing and containing it. Were it not that it were subdued and contained, it would devastate the fields and herds. Each conceals goodness and blessing. Whenever earth is ploughed and turned over, its blessing, goodness and fruit appear. So how does the one bear comparison to the other?

2. Allah the Mighty has made the earth the place of His House in which His name is mentioned and in which He is glorified morning and evening, and in particular His Sacred House which He has set up as an establishment for people, blessed, and made a guidance for the worlds. If it was only that His Sacred House was in the earth, that would have been a sufficient honour and boast over fire.

3. The nature of fire, in contrast to earth, is corruption and

destruction of whatever it attaches itself to.

4. Earth is necessary for living creatures. They have absolute need of it - what is formed of it and from it, whereas dumb animals have absolutely no need of fire and man has no need of it for days and months. Necessity does not compel him to it.

5. Because of his shortsightedness and weak insight, the accursed Iblis saw the form of clay as earth mixed with fire and disdained it. He did not know that clay is compounded of two basic substances: water, from which Allah makes every living thing, and earth, which He has made a treasure-house of benefits and blessings. If he had looked beyond the form of the clay to its substance and end, he would have seen that it is better than fire.

6. Furthermore, even if it were valid by some specious argument that fire was better than clay, it would not necessitate that what was created from fire would be better than what was created from clay. The One who has power over everything can create from an inferior substance something which is better than what He creates from the superior substance. One considers the perfection of the end not the imperfection of the subtance. The Accursed One could not look beyond the substance nor move beyond it to the perfection of the form and the good of the creation.

WHAT IS THE GREATEST GOAL OF SHAYTAN?

The greatest goal of Shaytan in which he expends all his efforts is to make the children of Adam enter the punishment of the Blaze. Allah says,

'He calls his party only that they may be among the inhabitants of the Blaze.' (35:6)

THE THINGS TO WHICH SHAYTAN CALLS MAN

The first thing which Shaytan desires from the slave is disbelief and associating things with Allah and antagonism to Allah and His Messenger. If he can obtain that from the son of Adam, his sighs abate and he can rest from his toil with him. Allah says,

'Like Shaytan when he said to man, "Disbelieve"; then, when he disbelieved, he said, "Surely I am quit of you." ' (59:16)

The Prophet, may Allah bless him and grant him peace, said, 'O people! Allah the Mighty has commanded me to teach you that of which you are ignorant. Part of what He has taught me on this day is: "All that My slave disregards is lawful for him. I created My slaves all rightly inclined. Then the shaytans came to them and made them unsteady and turned them from their deen. They command them to associate with Me that for which I have not sent down any authority." ' (*Muslim relates the like of it.*)

If Shaytan is unable to make people fall into associating things with Allah and into disbelief, he does not despair and is content with less than that. He makes them fall into innovation which he loves better than deviation and acts of rebellion because it contains greater harm for the deen.

Sufyan ath-Thawri said, 'Iblis prefers innovation to rebellion because one can repent from rebellion, but one cannot repent from innovation.'

When Shaytan cannot succeed in the ways already mentioned, he calls the sons of Adam to wrong actions and acts of rebellion, whether they are major or minor ones, as he does in planting enmity and hatred in the ranks of the Muslims.

Allah says,

'He only commands you to evil and outrage and that you should say things against Allah that you do not know.' (2:169)

Allah also says,

'Shaytan only desires to cause enmity and hatred between you in regard to wine and arrow-shuffling, and to bar you from the remembrance of Allah and from the prayer. Will you then desist?' (5:91)

The Prophet, may Allah bless him and grant him peace, said, 'Shaytan has despaired of ever being worshipped in this land of yours. But he is content to be obeyed in some of your actions which you think little of.' (*At- Tirmidhi and Ibn Majah relate it with a good isnad.*)

The Prophet, may Allah bless him and grant him peace, said, 'Shaytan has despaired of being worshipped by those who pray in the Arabian penisula, but he causes enmity and hatred between you.' (*Muslim relates it.*)

What we have already mentioned is not enough for Shaytan. He also discourages the believers from acts of obedience. The following hadith makes this clear:

The Messenger of Allah, may Allah bless him and grant him peace, said, 'Shaytan lies in ambush for the son of Adam on his paths. He sits in ambush for him on the path of Islam and says, "Are you going to become Muslim and leave your deen and the deen of your fathers and the fathers of your fathers?"

'He disobeys him and becomes Muslim. Then Shaytan sits in ambush for him on the path of hijra and says, "Are you making hijra and leaving your land and your sky? The emigrant is like a horse on a steep slope."

'He disobeys him and goes on hijra. Then he sits in ambush for him on the path of jihad and says, "Are you going out on jihad when it is troublesome for the self and property? You will fight and be killed and your wife will marry someone else and your property will be divided!"

'He disobeys him and goes on jihad.'

The Messenger of Allah, may Allah bless him and grant him peace, said, 'Whoever does that, it is a duty for Allah to let him enter the Garden. Whoever is killed, it is a duty for Allah to let him enter the Garden. If he drowns, it is a duty for Allah to let him enter the Garden. If his beast throws him and breaks his neck, it is a duty for Allah to let him enter the Garden.' (*An-Nasa'i transmits it from Sabra b. Abi Fakih.*)

The evidence for this exists in the Noble Qur'an when Allah says,

'Now, because You have sent me astray,
I will surely sit in ambush for them on Your straight path.
Then I shall come on them from before them
and from behind them,
from their right hands and their left hands.
You will not find most of them thankful.' (7:16-17)

Shaytan is not content with discouraging the slaves of Allah from performing acts of obedience, he also strives to corrupt their acts of obedience and worship. The Messenger of Allah, may Allah bless him and grant him peace, said, 'When Shaytan hears the call to prayer, he turns his back and breaks wind so as not to hear the sound of it. When it is finished, he returns and whispers. When he hears the *iqama*, he leaves so that he does not hear its sound. When it is finished, he returns and whispers.' One version has, 'When the *iqama* is finished, he advances so that he can whisper between a man and his soul. He says, "Remember such-and-such, remember such-and-such" which the man had not in mind before until he does not know how much he has prayed.' (*Muslim relates the like of it.*)

One of the Companions came to the Messenger and said, 'Shaytan comes between me and my prayer and my recitation and makes it confused for me.'

The Prophet, may Allah bless him and grant him peace, said, 'That is a shaytan called Khinzib. When you sense him, then seek refuge in Allah from him and spit to your left side three times.'

He said, 'I did that and Allah removed him from me.' (*Muslim transmits the hadith in the Sahih.*)

WHAT ACT OF REBELLION DOES IBLIS PREFER?

It is separating a man and his wife and family and causing separation between people in general. The answer to this question will be made clear to us in the following words of the Messenger of Allah, may Allah bless him and grant him peace, 'The throne of Iblis is on the sea. He sends out his armies to cause trouble between people. He increases the sedition which one of them brings who says, "I did such-and-such." He says, "That's nothing." Then one of them comes and says, "I did such-and-such." He says, "That's nothing." Then one of them comes and says, "I did not leave him until I parted him from his wife." He draws near him and says, "You did well." (*Muslim relates the like of it as we have already indicated.*)

THE JINN BRINGING DOWN A MAN AND ITS CURE

That the jinn can enter a human body, as Ibn Taimiyya says *Majmu' al-Fatawa,* [24:276], is established by the agreement of the Imams of the people of the sunna and the community. Allah says,

'Those who consume usury shall not rise again except as he rises, whom Shaytan prostrates by the touch.' (2:275)

In the Sahih, the Prophet, may Allah bless him and grant him peace, said, 'Shaytan runs through the son of Adam like blood.'

The jinn can bring a man down out of appetite and passion as one man will do to another. It mostly arises from hatred and getting one's own back - for instance a person might have harmed them or they think that people have deliberately harmed them, either by urinating or pouring boiling water on one of them, or killing one of them.

As we already stated, the jinn are slaves of Allah subject to His command and bound to worship according to the Shari'a. If a muslim can manage to speak to them, as is the case when the jinn bring down a man, he is under obligation to do that.

When the jinn bring down a man in the first way, out of appetite and passion, they do it by committing outrageous actions which Allah has forbidden men and jinn. Even if such actions seem pleasing, how can they really be pleasing when they amount to outrage and injustice. One reminds the jinn of that since they know that this is a forbidden action or outrage and enmity. The one who addresses them does this in order to establish the proof against them and so that they know the judgment of Allah and His Messenger whom He has sent to both jinn and men.

If it is from the second area, that is because of injury done to them by a human being and the person concerned was not aware of what he had done, the jinn are told that the man did not realize. Someone who does not cause harm deliberately does not deserve to be punished. If it happens in his own house and property, the jinn should know that a man's house is his property and he can do whatever is permitted in it, and that one cannot remain in the property of men and not be harmed by them. The jinn have their own places separate from the dwelling-places of men like ruins and open country.

Ibn Taimiyya says in *Majmu' al-Fatawa*, [29:42] , 'What is meant is that when the jinn attack a man, they are told about the judgment of Allah and His Messenger and the proof is established against them and they are commanded to do what is correct and forbidden the wrong as one does with men because Allah says,

"We never punish until We have sent a messenger." (17:15)

Allah also says,

**"Company of jinn and men,
did not messengers come to you from among you,
relating to you My signs and warning you
of the encounter of this day of yours?..." (6:130)**

THE JINN AND THE PLAGUE

The Messenger of Allah, may Allah bless him and grant him peace, said, 'My community will be destroyed by attack and the plague, which is the piercing of your enemies among the jinn. There is martyrdom in each.' (*Ahmad and at- Tabarani transmit it with a sound isnad.*)

It is related in the *Mustadrak* of al-Hakam, 'The plague is the piercing of your enemies among the jinn and it is martyrdom for you.'

Az-Zamakhshari says that the plague was called 'the spears of the jinn'.

Perhaps what befell the Prophet of Allah, Ayyub, was caused by the jinn as Allah says,

**'Remember Our slave Ayyub when he called to his Lord,
"Behold, Shaytan has touched me
with weariness and punishment." ' (38:41)**

FALSE MENSTRUATION IS FROM SHAYTAN

One of the illnesses with which Shaytan afflicts human women is false menstruation. The Messenger of Allah, may Allah bless him and grant him peace, said, 'It is an impulse from Shaytan.' (*At-Tirmidhi transmits it and thought it good.*)

SHAYTAN AND DREAMS

Shaytan tries constantly to cause harm to a man's body and being. He harms his body by illnesses. He harms his being by various means. One of them worth mentioning is dreams.

Shaytan shows man troublesome dreams in his sleep with the aim of causing him sorrow and psychological trouble. The Prophet, may Allah bless him and grant him peace, reported that 'There are three types of dreams which a man sees in his sleep: the vision from the Merciful, the dream which causes sorrow from Shaytan and the dream which is the chatter of the self.' (*Muslim relates something similar.*)

The Prophet, may Allah bless him and grant him peace, said, 'When one of you has a dream he likes, it is from Allah so he should praise Allah for it and relate it. If he sees something else which he dislikes, it is from Shaytan so he should seek refuge from its evil and not mention it to anyone. Then it will not harm him.' (*Al-Bukhari relates it.*)

THE WHISPERING OF SHAYTAN

The meaning of the verbal root from which the word 'whispering' comes, is the movement and the low voice which one does not perceive so that one can be on guard against it. Whispering is a hidden casting into the self.

But how does Iblis whisper and how does that whispering reach the heart?

Ibn 'Aqil, in answer to this question, said, 'It consists of words to which the self and nature inclines. It is said that he enters into the body of the son of Adam because he is a subtle body, and whispers. He provokes the self with base thoughts. Allah says, "He whispers in the breasts of men." '

Some people say that this statement is not sound because two parts of it are false. They point out that Iblis' speech can be heard by the physical ears. As for his entering into bodies, bodies do not intermix. Furthermore, because he is fire, he must burn man. It is said that his speech could refer to something to which the self inclines, for example, like the sorcerer who spits at the bewitched, even though that is not a voice.

As for the statement that if Iblis had been able to enter a man, bodies would intermix and the man would be burned - that is mistaken because the jinn are not made of fire that burns. They were created from fire in their origin. As for the statement that bodies do not intermix, the subtle body can enter into the dense body like the spirit or the air which penetrates all bodies. The jinn have subtle bodies.

HASTE IS FROM SHAYTAN

Ibn as-Sunni related in Al-Ijaz that the Messenger of Allah, may Allah bless him and grant him peace, said, 'Deliberation is from Allah, the Mighty and Majestic, and haste is from Shaytan.'

SHAYTAN CLINGS TO THE UNJUST JUDGE

There is no doubt that the unjust judge does not deserve the company of Allah. The company which he deserves is the company of Shaytan. It is that which is fitting for him. The Messenger of Allah, may Allah bless him and grant him peace, said, 'Allah is with the Qadi as long as he is not unjust. When he is unjust, He leaves him and Shaytan clings to him.' (*At-Tirmidhi relates it from the hadith of 'Abdullah b. Abi Awfa*).

SHAYTAN BINDING THE HEAD OF THE SLEEPER

The Messenger of Allah, may Allah bless him and grant him peace, said, 'Shaytan ties three knots on the neck of one of you when he sleeps. He ties each knot on you in the long night and goes to sleep. If you awaken and remember Allah, the Mighty and Majestic, one knot is undone. If you do wudu', another knot is undone. If you pray, another knot is undone. Then you get up active and cheerful. If not you wake up lazy and grouchy.' (*Al- Bukhari relates it.*)

This occurs to the one who has not recited the *Ayat al-Kursi* or the end of *Sura al-Baqara* or any part of the Qur'an which will protect him from the shaytans. As for the person who has recited such things, Shaytan has no way to get at him, as is proven by the hadiths which will come at the end of the book, Allah willing.

SHAYTAN TOUCHING MAN

The Messenger of Allah, may Allah bless him and grant him peace, said, 'Shaytan has a touch on the son of Adam and the angel also has a touch. The touch of Shaytan threatens evil and rejection of the truth. The touch of the angel promises good and confirmation of the truth. Whoever experiences that should know that it is from Allah, the Mighty, and should praise Allah. Whoever experiences the first, should seek refuge in Allah from Shaytan and then recite, "Shaytan promises you poverty and commands you to outrageous action." ' (*Al-Tirmidhi transmits it.*)

SHAYTAN IS PRESENT WHEN A CHILD IS BORN

No child is born without Shaytan being present - except for Maryam and her son. In the hadith of Abu Hurayra found in both the *Sahih* of Muslim and of al-Bukhari, the Messenger of Allah, may Allah bless him and grant him peace, said, 'There is no son of Adam born except that Shaytan pricks him. He begins to yell because he has pricked him - except for Maryam and her son.'

SHAYTAN'S PRESENCE DURING INTERCOURSE

Shaytan is present when a man has intercourse with his wife, which is why the Muslim must mention Allah then and also seek refuge from Shaytan.

It is confirmed in both the Sahih of Muslim and of al-Bukhari that the Messenger of Allah, may Allah bless him and grant him peace, said, 'When one of you wants to go to his wife, he should say, "In the name of Allah. O Allah, protect us from Shaytan and keep Shaytan from what we are provided with." Then if a child is decreed for them at that time, Shaytan will never harm him.'

SHAYTAN'S PRESENCE IN ALL THE AFFAIRS OF MAN

Shaytan is present in all human affairs. Muslim and al-Tirmidhi relate the hadith from Jabir that the Messenger of Allah, may Allah bless him and grant him peace, said, 'Shaytan is present in all you do. He is even present when you eat. When you drop a morsel, he takes it. One should clean it off and eat it and not leave it for Shaytan. When you finish, you should lick your fingers. No-one knows in which part of his food the blessing lies.'

CHAPTER EIGHT

MAN'S WEAPONS AGAINST SHAYTAN

Comprising:

Seeking refuge with Allah.
Seeking refuge when reciting the Qur'an.
Seeking refuge when entering the lavatory.
Seeking refuge when going to sleep.
The two suras of seeking refuge.
Remembering Allah often.
The first three ayats of Sura Ghafir together with the Ayat al-Kursi.
The end of Sura al-Baqara.
Wudu' and the prayer.
Recitation of the Ayat al-Kursi.
Repentance and asking forgiveness.
Reciting Sura al-Baqara.
Refraining from excess.
The fortress of knowledge.
Clinging to the Muslim community.

SEEKING REFUGE WITH ALLAH

One of the early scholars asked a student of his the question, 'What do you do about Shaytan when he tries to entice you into error?'

The student replied, 'I struggle with him.'

'And if he does it again?'

The student said, 'I struggle with him.'

'This goes on and on,' the teacher said. 'What would you do if you passed by some sheep and the sheepdog kept barking at you and kept you from continuing on your way?'

He replied, 'I would keep on until I drove him off.'

'That would take too much time,' the teacher said. 'You should ask the shepherd's help in keeping the dog away from you!'

The best source of help against Shaytan is the One who created Shaytan! And the best way to protect oneself from Shaytan and his troops is to seek refuge and protection in Allah. He has power over him, and if He protects His slave, how can Shaytan get at him?

Allah says,

'Take forgiveness and command what is correct
and turn away from the ignorant.
If a provocation from Shaytan provokes you,
then seek refuge in Allah.
He is Hearing, Knowing.' (7:199-200)

Allah the Mighty commands His Messenger and every believer to seek refuge in Him from the promptings and presence of the shaytans,

'Say: O my Lord, I take refuge with You
from the promptings of the shaytans
and I seek refuge with You lest they be present with me.'
(23:97-98)

If you wish to know what seeking refuge means, then according to Ibn Kathir in his *Tafsir*, it is to seek protection in Allah the Mighty from the evil of everything evil. 'I seek refuge with Allah from the Accursed Shaytan' means 'I seek protection with Allah from the Accursed Shaytan so that he does not harm me in my deen and worldly affairs or prevent me from doing what I am commanded or draw me into doing what I have been forbidden.' Only Allah can protect man from Shaytan. That is why Allah commands Shaytan to entice and flatter man by offering him beautiful things so as to make him overlook the harm in them and He commands people to seek refuge in Him from the Shaytan of the jinn because Shaytan does not accept bribes nor does the beautiful affect him because he is evil by nature. Only the One who created him can avert him from you.

It says in a hadith that 'Abdu'r-Rahman b. Khanaysh was asked whether he met the Prophet, may Allah bless him and grant him peace. When he replied that he had, he was asked what the Messenger of Allah, may Allah bless him and grant him peace, did on the night when the shaytans attacked him. He said, 'The shaytans came down that night on the Messenger of Allah from the valleys and canyons, including a shaytan holding a fire-brand. He wanted to burn the face of the Messenger of Allah, may Allah bless him and grant him peace, with it. Jibril, peace be upon him, came down to him and said, "O Muhammad, speak!" He said, "What should I say?"

'Jibril replied, "Say: I seek refuge with the perfect words of Allah from the evil of what He has created, and from the evil of what descends from heaven and from the evil of what rises in it, and from the evil of the night and the day, and from the evil of every visitor except a visitor who brings good, O Merciful!" '

'Abdu'r-Rahman continued, 'Their fire was extinguished and Allah defeated them.' (*Ahmad b. Hanbal transmits it.*)

SEEKING REFUGE WHEN RECITING THE QUR'AN

Allah commmands people to seek refuge when they recite the Qur'an. He says,

'When you recite the Qur'an,
seek refuge from the accursed Shaytan.
He has no power over those who believe and trust in their Lord.'
(16:98-99)

Seeking refuge with Allah from Shaytan when you recite the Qur'an has much benefit and wisdom:

1. The Qur'an is healing for what is in the breasts of men. It removes the whisperings, appetites and false desires which Shaytan casts in them. It is medicine against what Shaytan commands.

This healing medicine works on the heart when it is free of conflict and opposition to it.

2. The Qur'an sustains guidance, knowledge, and good in the heart just as water sustains plants, whereas Shaytan is fire which consumes plants bit by bit. Whenever he senses good in the heart, he strives to corrupt and burn it. The reciter of Qur'an is commanded to seek refuge in Allah from Shaytan so that he will not corrupt what the reciter has gained by his recitation.

The difference between this aspect and the previous one is that in the first one seeking refuge is to gain the benefit of the Qur'an and in the second one it is to maintain and guard it.

3. The angels draw near to the one who recites the Qur'an and listen to his recitation. For instance it is mentioned that when Usayd b. Hufayr was reciting, he saw something like a canopy full of lamps. The Prophet, peace and blessings be upon him, told him, 'Those were angels.'

The rest of the hadith is in al-Bukhari, 'Those angels drew near to your voice. If you had continued reciting, the people would have looked at them in the morning and they would not have concealed themselves from them.'

Shaytan is the opponent and enemy of the angels. Therefore the reciter of Qur'an is commanded to ask Allah to put his enemy far away so that His angels can be with him. The angels and shaytans cannot be together in such circumstances.

4. Shaytan rallies his troops of horsemen and his footmen against the reciter of Qur'an until he distracts him from his purpose in reciting the Qur'an, namely reflection, understanding and the knowledge of what the Speaker wants to say. He tries hard to come between his heart and the goal of the Qur'an so that the reciter does not derive full benefit from it. Therefore he is commanded at the beginning to seek refuge with Allah from the accursed Shaytan.

5. The reciter of Qur'an is conversing with Allah with His own words. Allah listens more attentively to someone with a good voice reciting the Qur'an than the owner of a singing slavegirl listens to her singing. Shaytan's recitation is poetry and singing. The reciter is commanded to drive Shaytan off by seeking refuge when he converses with Allah and his Lord is listening to his recitation.

6. Allah states that He has not sent any Messenger or Prophet but that Shaytan 'cast into his fancy when he was fancying' (22:52). All the *Salaf* say that this means when he recites, Shaytan casts something into his recitation. If he does this with the Messengers, peace

and blessings be upon them, then why not with other people? This is why the reciter of Qur'an sometimes errs and his recitation becomes confused and muddled for him - that is either on the tongue or his mind and heart are confused about it, and when he is in the process of reciting, he does not like this or that in it. Sometimes the two happen together.

7. Shaytan is never so covetous towards man as when he is concerned with good or sets about doing it. Then he is fierce in his efforts to cut him off from it.[1]

SEEKING REFUGE WHEN ENTERING THE LAVATORY

The sunna is that when you enter the lavatory, you should seek refuge with Allah from Shaytan, as reported in the *Sahih* of Muslim and al-Bukhari. Anas said that when the Prophet, may Allah bless him and grant him peace, entered the lavatory, he said, 'O Allah, I seek refuge with you from the male and female shaytans.'

In the *Sunan* of Abu Da'ud there is a hadith with a sound isnad in which Zayd b. Arqam says that the Messenger of Allah, may Allah bless him and grant him peace, said, 'These privies are peopled with jinn, so when one of you goes to the lavatory, he should say, "I seek refuge in Allah from male and female shaytans." '

SEEKING REFUGE WHEN GOING TO SLEEP

It is recommended to seek refuge when going to sleep as has been related in the *Musnad* of Ahmad b. Hanbal from Muhammad b. Ishaq from 'Amr b. Shu'ayb from his father that his grandfather said, 'The Messenger of Allah, may Allah bless him and grant him peace, taught us some words to say when going to sleep: "In the name of Allah. I seek refuge in the perfect words of Allah from His anger, His punishment, the evil of His slaves and from the spurrings of the shaytans and from their being present." '

THE TWO SURAS OF SEEKING REFUGE

The best way to seek refuge is reciting the best verses of seeking refuge, *al-Falaq* (113) and *an-Nas* (114). 'Uqba b. 'Amir said that the Messenger of Allah, may Allah bless him and grant him peace, said, 'No-one can seek refuge with anything as effectively as with, "Say, I

[1] Imam Ibn al-Qayyim, Ighatha al-Lahfan, 1:109.

seek refuge in the Lord of the Dawn" and "Say, I seek refuge in the Lord of men." '

Their excellence has been reported in many other hadiths. One of them is that related by Muslim from 'Uqba b. 'Amir who says that the Messenger of Allah, may Allah bless him and grant him peace, said, 'Do you not see that verses have been sent down tonight whose like has never been seen? That is, "Say, I seek refuge in the Lord of the Dawn" and "Say, I seek refuge in the Lord of men." '

Ahmad related that the Messenger of Allah said to him, 'Shall I tell you the best thing to use for seeking refuge?' 'Yes,' he replied. The Prophet said, "Say, I seek refuge in the Lord of the Dawn" and "Say, I seek refuge in the Lord of men." '

At-Tirmidhi transmits from Abu Hurayra that Abu Sa'id said, 'The Messenger of Allah, may Allah bless him and grant him peace, used to seek refuge from the jinn and the evil eye of men until the two suras of seeking refuge were revealed. When they were revealed, he used them and abandoned other ways.'

REMEMBERING ALLAH OFTEN

What do you think of a man whose enemies have encircled him with malicious intent? They have him surrounded and each of them can do him whatever evil and harm they so desire. There is no way he can throw them off except by remembering Allah.

Remembrance of Allah according to Ibn al-Qayyim in Al-Wasil as-Sayyib is the greatest rescuer of the slave from Shaytan, 'If Remembrance only possessed this one single quality, it would be proper for the slave to never let his tongue cease from remembering Allah.'

I will recount a hadith to the noble reader to remind him of the benefit which Allah has placed in Remembrance. 'Abdu'r-Rahman b. Samura said, 'The Messenger of Allah, may Allah bless him and grant him peace, came out to us one day when we were in the *Suffa* in Madina. He approached us and said, "I saw something wondrous yesterday. I saw a man of my community to whom the Angel of Death was coming to take his soul. His dutifulness to his parents came and turned the Angel of Death from him.

"I saw a man who was being racked by the punishment of the grave and his wudu' came and rescued him from that.

"I saw a man of my community surrounded by shaytans. Remembrance of Allah came and drove the shaytans away from him.

"I saw a man of my community surrounded by the Angels of Punishment. His prayer came and rescued him from their hands.

"I saw a man of my community panting from thirst. Whenever he drew near to a basin, he was kept from it and driven off. His fasting the month of Ramadan came and gave him water, quenching his thirst.

"I saw a man of my community and I saw the prophets sitting in circles. Whenever he drew near to a circle,he was driven off. His ablution from major impurity (*janaba*) came and took him by the hand and let him sit beside me.

"I saw a man from my community with darkness in front of him, darkness behind him, darkness on his left, darkness on his right, darkness above him and darkness below him. He was stumbling in confusion. His Hajj and *'Umra* came and brought him out of the darkness into the light.

"I saw a man from my community trying to protect himself from the heat and sparks of the Fire. His charity came and became a veil between him and the Fire and it shaded his head.

"I saw a man from my community speaking to the believers who ignored him. His maintaining ties of kinship came and said, 'O company of Muslims! He maintained ties of kinship, so speak to him.' Then the believers spoke to him and shook his hand.

"I saw a man from my community encircled by the *Zabaniyya* (angels who guard the Fire). His commanding the correct and forbidding the wrong came and rescued him from their hands and brought him to the angels of mercy.

I saw a man from my community kneeling with a veil between him and Allah. His good character came, took him by the hand and brought him to Allah, the Mighty and Majestic.

"I saw a man from my community whose page had been placed in his left hand. His fear of Allah came and took his page and placed it in his right hand.

"I saw a man from my community who was light in the balance. His children who had died before him came and made his balance heavy.

"I saw a man from my community standing on the brink of the Fire. His hope in Allah came and rescued him.

"I saw a man from my community who had fallen in the Fire. The tears which he had wept out of fear of Allah came and rescued him.

"I saw a man from my community standing on the *Sirat* shaking like a leaf in a gale. His good opinion of Allah came and stilled his terror.

"I saw a man from my community crawling across the *Sirat*, sometimes inching along, sometimes frozen. His prayer came and stood him upright and saved him.

"I saw a man from my community who had reached the gates of the Garden which were locked against him. His testimony of 'There is no god but Allah' came and opened the gates for him and let him enter the Garden." '

Abu Musa al-Madini relates this hadith in the Book *At-Targhib fi'l-Khisal al-Munjiyya wa't-Tarhib min al-Khilal al-Murdiyya*. He says that it is a very good hadith.

According to Ibn al-Qayyim, the Shaykh al-Islam, Ibn Taimiyya, thought this hadith very important. I have heard that he used to say, 'There is testimony to its soundness.' He meant the words of the Prophet, may Allah bless him and grant him peace, 'I saw a man from my community encircled by the shaytans. His Remembrance of Allah came and drove the shaytans from him.'

Remembrance of Allah is the greatest rescuer of the slave from Shaytan! Perhaps this will become yet clearer by mentioning the hadith in which the Prophet of Allah, Yahya, when ordering the Banu Isra'il to have five qualities, commanded them to remember Allah the Great, saying that the example of it was that of a man hotly pursued by an enemy who comes to a fortified fortress and protects himself from him. Similarly, the slave can only protect himself from Shaytan by remembering Allah.

The benefits of being occupied with remembrance of Allah are innumerable. There is not enough room here to go further into it. If the reader desires to learn more about these benefits, he should refer to the book by Imam al- Ghazzali *Al-Adhkar wa'd-Du'awat* edited by Muhammad al-Khasht, and *Al-Wabil as-Sayyib min al-Kalam at-Tayyib* by Ibn al-Qayyim.

THE FIRST THREE AYATS OF *SURA GHAFIR* TOGETHER WITH THE *AYAT AL-KURSI*

These ayats of *Sura Ghafir* are:

'Ha Mim. The sending-down of the Book is from Allah, the Mighty, the Knowing, Forgiver of wrong actions, Accepter of repentance, Terrible in Retribution, the Bountiful. There is no god but He and to Him is the homecoming.' (40:1-3)

This is recited together with the *Ayat al-Kursi* (2:255).

At-Tirmidhi transmits from Abu Hurayra that the Messenger of Allah, may Allah bless him and grant him peace, said, 'If someone recites the passage from "Ha Mim" to "the homecoming" from Sura al-Mu'min together with the Throne Verse in the morning, he is protected by them until the evening. If someone recites them in the evening, he is protected by them until morning.'

THE END OF SURA AL-BAQARA

At-Tirmidhi relates that Abu Mas'ud al-Ansari reported that the Messenger of Allah, may Allah bless him and grant him peace, said, 'Someone who recites the two ayats at the end of *Sura al-Baqara* at night averts harm from himself.'

At-Tirmidhi relates that an-Nu'man b. Bashir said that the Prophet, may Allah bless him and grant him peace, said, 'Two thousand years before creating Creation, Allah wrote a book from which He has sent down two verses with which He concludes *Sura al-Baqara*. Shaytan will not come near a house in which they are recited for three nights.'

WUDU' AND THE PRAYER

Wudu' and the prayer are among man's greatest protections against Shaytan, especially against the force of anger and appetite, which is a cauldron simmering in the heart of the son of Adam.

At-Tirmidhi relates from Abu Sa'id al-Khudri that the Prophet, may Allah bless him and grant him peace, said, 'Anger is a glowing coal in the heart of the son of Adam, haven't you seen the redness of his eyes and the swelling of his jugular veins? If someone feels its touch, he should sit on the earth.'

Ahmad b. Hanbal transmits that 'Atiyya b. 'Urwa said that the Messenger of Allah, may Allah bless him and grant him peace, said, 'Anger is from Shaytan and Shaytan was created from fire. Fire is extinguished by water, so when one of you becomes angry, he should do wudu'.

RECITATION OF THE AYAT AL-KURSI

Reciting the *Ayat al-Kursi* is the best protection the son of Adam has from Shaytan. In the *Sahih* there is the hadith of Muhammad b. Sirin in which Abu Hurayra says, 'The Messenger of Allah, may Allah bless him and grant him peace, put me in charge of guarding the zakat of Ramadan. Then someone came up to me and began to take handfuls of the food. I grabbed him and said, "I am going to take you before the Messenger of Allah, may Allah bless him and grant him peace" ' - the hadith goes on at some length until the intruder tells him, 'When you go to your bed, recite the *Ayat al-Kursi.* Allah will send down a guardian over you and no shaytan will come near you until morning.' The Prophet, may Allah bless him and grant him peace, said, 'He has told you the truth although he is a great liar. That was Shaytan.'

REPENTANCE AND ASKING FORGIVENESS

One of the greatest things with which the believer can confront Shaytan is to quickly repent and return to Allah when Shaytan makes him err. This is the state of the right-acting slaves of Allah. Allah says,

'Those who fear Allah,
when a visitation of Shaytan touches them, remember,
and then they see clearly.' (7:201)

Al-Hakam and Ahmad b. Hanbal transmit that the Messenger of Allah mentioned that Shaytan said to the Lord of Might, 'By Your might, O Lord, I will pervert Your slaves as long as their souls are in their bodies!' The Lord said, 'By My might and My majesty, I will continue to forgive them as long as they ask for My forgiveness.'

RECITING SURA AL-BAQARA

Reciting *Sura al-Baqara* (2) will put the shaytans far from the Muslim and his house. The Messenger of Allah, may Allah bless him and grant him peace, said, 'Do not make your houses into graves. Shaytan does not enter a house in which Al-Baqara is recited.'

Ahmad b. Hanbal relates a similar hadith from Suhayl from his father from Abu Hurayra:

'There is no god but Allah alone with no partner. He has the Kingdom and He has the praise and He has power over everything.' If the Muslim repeats this a hundred times it will bring him many fruits. This is made clear by the words of the Messenger of Allah, may Allah bless him and grant him peace, 'If someone says, "There is no god but Allah alone with no partner. He has the Kingdom and He has the praise and He has power over everything." a hundred times in a day he will gain the equivalent of freeing ten slaves and a hundred good actions are written for him and a hundred bad actions are wiped out for him and it is a protection for him against Shaytan for that day until the evening. No one will bring anything more excellent than what he brings except a man who has done more than he has.'

The hadith is in the *Sahih* collections of al-Bukhari and Muslim in the hadith of Samura, the client of Abu Bakr, from Abu Salih from Abu Hurayra.

REFRAINING FROM EXCESS

Amongst the things that will keep the believer far from falling into the snares of Shaytan is to refrain from excess in glances, words, food and socializing with people. By these four doors Shaytan gains power over the son of Adam and obtains what he wants from him.

As for looking, the Messenger of Allah, may Allah bless him and grant him peace, said, 'Do not follow a glance with a glance. You are allowed the first but not the second.' (*Ahmad b. Hanbal transmits it in the Musnad.*)

As for excess words, the Prophet, may Allah bless him and grant him peace, said, 'Part of the excellence of a man's Islam is that he leaves what does not concern him.' (*Ahmad relates it.*)

As for excess food, the Prophet, may Allah bless him and grant him peace, said, 'A man does not fill a worse vessel than his belly.' (*Ahmad relates it.*)

Luqman the Sage used to say to his son, 'My son, when the intestines are full, reflection goes to sleep, wisdom falls silent, and the limbs cease to worship.'

As for excessive socializing, it is a chronic disease which attracts evil. How frequently are socializing and company empty of blessing! How often do they sow enmity! How often they plant rancour in the heart and as long as it remains in the heart it erodes firm mountains of good actions! Excessive socializing contains loss for this world and the Next World. The slave must only indulge in that amount of socializing which is necessary.

THE FORTRESS OF KNOWLEDGE

One of the greatest fortresses which protects the believer against Shaytan is knowledge.

The Messenger of Allah, may Allah bless him and grant him peace, said, 'One faqih is stronger against Shaytan than a thousand worshippers.' (*At-Tirmidhi transmits it.*)

The importance of knowledge for the believer in opposing Shaytan is well illustrated by the following story related by Ibn 'Abbas:

'The shaytans say to Iblis, "Master, we delight in the death of a man of knowledge more than we rejoice in that of a man of worship. We are harmed by the man of knowledge, but not harmed by the man of worship."

'Iblis says, "Come on, let's go." So off they go to a man of worship and come to him while he is worshipping and tell him they want to ask him a question. Iblis says, "Can your Lord put this world inside an egg?"

'The worshipper replies, "I don't know."

'Iblis says to the shaytans, "Don't you see there is disbelief in his answer?"

'They then go to a man of knowledge in his circle joking with his companions and say, "We want to ask you a question."

'He says, "Ask." so Iblis says to him, "Can your Lord put this world inside an egg?"

'He replies, "Yes."

'Iblis asks, "How?"

'The man of knowledge says,

"His command when He desires a thing is that He says to it, 'Be!' and it is." (36:82)

'Iblis says to the shaytans, "Don't you see that that man (the worshipper) does not have any effect beyond himself while this man (the man of knowledge) estranges much of the world from me?" '

CLINGING TO THE MUSLIM COMMUNITY

It is well known that Shaytan is with those who oppose the community. For that reason, the Muslim must keep to the Muslim community because that will keep him far from the errors and snares of Shaytan.

The Messenger of Allah, may Allah bless him and grant him peace, said, 'Whoever of you desires the heart of the Garden should cling to the community. Shaytan is with the solitary person and further off from a couple.' (*At-Tirmidhi and Ahmad ibn Hanbal transmit it. At-Tirmidhi says that it is a sound good hadith.*)

The Messenger of Allah, may Allah bless him and grant him peace, also said, 'The hand of Allah is over the community. Shaytan is with the one who opposes the community.' (*Ibn Sa'id transmits it.*)

GLOSSARY

Ayat: Verse of the Qur'an.

Dar al-Nadwa: Council chamber of the people of Makka.

Deen: Religion - way of life.

Faqih: Someone learned in religious matters.

Hadith: A direct report of what the Prophet Muhammad, peace be upon him, said or did.

Hijra: Emigration in the way of Allah.

Iblis: Proper name of Satan.

'Ifrit: A powerful kind of jinn.

Imam: Leader - particularly leader of the prayer.

Iqama: Call to prayer made immediately before the prayer is done.

Isnad: Chain of transmission.

Jahannam: One of the names of Hell.

Kharijites: A sect who believed that committing major wrong actions turns a Muslim into an unbeliever.

Marfu' hadith: A hadith which can only be traced back to a Companion of the Prophet.

Murji'ites: A sect who believed that a person's Islam was not affected by anything he did.

Qadi: A judge.

Qadiri: A sect who believed in the doctrine of human free will.

Qibla: Direction of Makka to be faced when praying.

Rafidites: A sect who rejected the first three khalifs of Islam.

Sahih: Faultless - used to refer to the most authentic books of hadith.

Salaf: First generation of Muslims.

Shaytan: Satan or one of Satan's agents.

Sirat: The knife – edged bridge that must be crossed to enter the Garden.

Suffa: A veranda attached to the Prophet's mosque in Madina where poor Muslims used to sleep.

Sunan: Books containing a record of sayings and sunna of the Prophet.

Sunna: Actions of the Prophet and his Companions taken as a model for subsequent generations.

Sura: A chapter of the Qur'an.

'Umra: The visit to the Ka'ba done outside the rites of Hajj.

Wudu': Purification by washing the limbs before prayer.

Zakat: Poor tax which every wealthy Muslim must pay.